CORDOBA

in focus

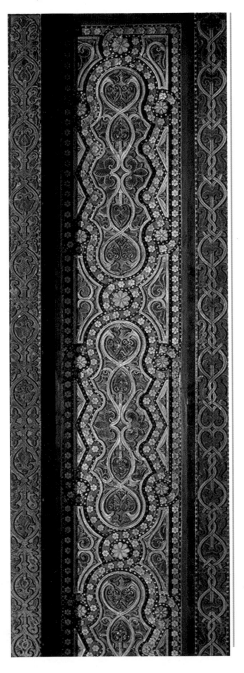

Córdoba is not a decadent town, one of those haughty cities languishing in its own past, in which life becomes stifled (...) it maintains its own elegant poise, made of the web of dreams and the substance of time itself ...; there are places here which seem to contain the entire essence of the universe hidden and untouched.

Antonio Muñoz Molina

Because of its strategic position in the Guadalquivir valley, Córdoba has always played a vital role in the history of Andalucía. In ancient times the river Guadalquivir was navigable right up to the town and provided a route via which all of the peoples who arrived in this southern-most point of Europe could enter and enrich the land with their traditions, trade and culture. On their way northwards to the higher mesetas of the Iberian peninsula they often stayed here and made the site of present-day Córdoba a base for administration, a place where they could exploit the agricultural possibilities of the terrain and the mineral resources of the hills. These peoples, long since gone, have often left behind them ample evidence of their passing in the archaeological remains of their settlements, which reveal highly successful and vigorous populations during the late bronze age, including that of Corduba, whose name has been translated by scholars to mean "Village overlooking the river". It must have been a relatively small settlement in modern terms but could already boast paved streets and a port on the river to cater for the growing trade throughout Andalucía. Finds have come to light of pottery and smelting ovens to make bronze from the copper and tin mined in the mountains above the town. Later the Iberian Tartessos formed a thriving community here and the

•ÉCIJA. SEVILLA

CORDOBA

SEVILLA

HUELVA

Phoenicians traded olive oil and salted fish in the region. But it was with the Roman occupation of the Iberian peninsula that the history of modern Córdoba really began and the town came to occupy a crucial position in the development of the whole of southern Spain. The region of Andalucía shares all the geographical reliefs and climatic features of an entire subcontinent.

MALA

CADIZ

•PUNTA UMBRÍA HUELVA

•CONIL-BARBATE. CA

Western or "lower" Andalucía is centred around the great valley of the river Guadalquivir, bordered by the mountains of the Sierra Morena to the north, and the Betic mountain chains to the south and east, and open to Atlantic winds from the south-west. Eastern, or "higher", Andalucia is dominated by the steep terrain and valleys of the Intrabetic mountain chains, above all the Sierra Nevada and the Sierra Fílabre. The Province of Córdoba occupies the heart of Andalucía and straddles the two basic geographical zones; Within this geographical and commercial context it is not hard to understand why Córdoba should have

•CASTLE DE BELALCÁZAR. CÓRDOBA

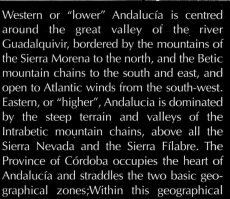

•CASTLE OF ALCAUDETE. JAÉN

become the most important city in Europe in the X century, comparable only to Baghdad or Constantinople in the East, a seat of learning, which nurtured the knowledge salvaged from classical antiquity that had been lost during the Dark Ages in Europe and without a revival of which the development of modern society would have been difficult to imagine.

• THE TABERNAS DESERT IN ALMERÍA.

•SIERRA NEVADA. GRANADA

•CÓMPETA. MÁLAGA

CORDOBA

in focus

THE HISTORY OF CORDOBA
THE CITY

• **A VIEW OF CÓRDO-BA** *drawn by Anton van den Wyngaerde in 1568*

• **LITHOGRAPH OF THE BRIDGE GATE**

• **SENECA.** *Lucius Annaeus Seneca (4 – 65 A.D.) was born into an aristocratic Córdoban family and became one of the foremost philosophers of Roman times.*

THE HISTORY OF CORDOBA

The Romans first arrived in Corduba, as it was known at that time, in 206 B.C. and made it an official colony in 169 B.C. Patrician Roman families soon settled there and in 152 B.C. it became the capital of Baetica, or Lower Hispania. In 45 B.C. more than 20,000 of its inhabitants were slain by Julius Caesar for supporting the sons of Pompey in the Roman civil war but the city managed to maintain its power in the region until the emperor Diocletian moved the capital to Hispalis (modern-day Sevilla) during the third century A.D. One illustrious son of Córdoba was Nero's tutor, Seneca, the stoic philosopher whose ideas embodied the spirit of the Andalucían people and whose atti-

• **THE TEMPLE OF CLAUDIUS MARCELLUS.** *The columns now standing in front of the town hall were reconstructed from a Roman temple.*

tudes became quintessential to popular belief. Other famous sons of the city were the poet Lucan and the early Christian bishop Hosius. Córdoba was virtually destroyed when barbarian tribes invaded from northern Europe in the V century but recovered slowly until in 711 Arabs from North Africa ousted a weakened Visigothic monarchy and five years later made Córdoba the capital of al-Andalus. This was the beginning of a new period of splendour, particularly from 756 onwards when Abd ar-Rahman I, the last survivor of the Umayyad dynasty from Damascus, the rest of whom had been wiped out by the rival Abbasid family, founded here a new dynasty and independent emirate. The new emir set up in Córdoba a strong, centralised state, not based upon the old desert tribal regimes, where each new ruler was elected by vote amongst the elders, but rather upon a power base of trade and commerce, thus paving the way for the succession of his own

V A

descendants to the throne, the most important of whom was to be Abd ar-Rahman III. At the beginning of the X century Abd ar-Rahman III managed to stifle the endemic spirit of revolt among the local populace and in 929 he took to himself the title of caliph and extended his power throughout the

• A FOREST OF CO-LUMNS IN THE GREAT MOSQUE.

•MADINAT AZ-ZAHRA *Abd ar-Rahman III built this royal city some eight kilometres from Córdoba for his favourite, Azahara. (936-1010)*

Iberian peninsula and much of North Africa. With the new caliphate, independent of Baghdad, Córdoba's period of greatest splendour began and lasted for more than 100 years. The caliph renovated and added considerably to the Great Mosque, founded by his forbear Abd ar-Rahman I in 784 and extended by Abd ar-Rahman II in 833. At vast expense he also began to build Madinat az-Zahra, the richest and most luxurious royal city the western world had ever seen. When Abd ar-Rahman III died in 961 his son al-Hakan II continued with the work on these great building projects. At this time Córdoba probably equalled Constantinople and Baghdad in wealth and power; it was famous for its libraries and scholars and is said to have contained at its height 3,000 mosques and

• A MANUSCRIPT *from the library that existed in Córdoba during the caliphate of al-Hakan II.*

• THE CALIPH ABD AR-RAHMAN III *consolidated the prosperity and prestige of the caliphate which he himself founded. Left: two likenesses of the caliph, both made after his death.*

- **AVERROËS** *(born Córdoba1126, died Marrakech 1198), renowned for his treatises upon medicine, mathematics and astronomy, but above all for his philosophical works.*

- **MAIMONIDES** *(born Córdoba 1135, died Egypt 1204), a great Jewish scholar, philosopher and physician. At the age of twenty-three he was forced to flee with his family to Fez to escape religious persecution at the hands of the fanatical Almohads in al-Andalus.*

100,000 shops. Al-Hakan's throne was usurped by the general Abu Amir Muhammad al-Mansur, who completed the construction of the Great Mosque and other public works, but by appointing a series of mediocre generals to positions of high office by 1013 had led the caliphate into inaplent ruin by 1031 its territories had disintegrated into a series of petty kingdoms known as *taifas*.

INTELLECTUAL APOGEE. As is wont to occur, political decline is often accompanied by an upsurge in learning and intellectual enquiry. The fall of the caliphate saw the appearance of such renowned and influential figures in western scholarship as the poet ibn Hazam (994 – 1064), the philosopher and jurist Averroës (1126 – 1198) and the Jewish theologian and physician Moses ben Maimon, otherwise known as Maimonides (1135 – 1204), who wrote, among many influential works, the *Mishne Torah*, a learned commentary on the Jewish code of law.

Among the *taifa* kingdoms the most important was that of Sevilla. This kingdom eventually absorbed Córdoba into its realm and its ruler al-Mutamid was about to restore the caliphate when once again intrigue, internal feuding and constant harassment from the Christian kingdoms to the north ruined his plans and prompted an invasion of the peninsula in about 1085 by the Almoravids, a fanatical north-African desert tribe, which set back the Christian advance on the south by some two centuries.

• THE SCIENTIFIC LEGACY OF AL-ANDALUS, *gleaned during the middle ages from the learning of the classical world, was fundamental to the rebirth of learning in the west after the dark ages. Averroës, for example, introduced Aristotle's philosophical ideas to the Christian world and his metaphysical thought, which he brought to Rome and Toledo, served as the basis for philosophical perspecti ✝ ves that have sur ✝ vived to this day.*

•HISTORICAL DOCUMENTS

There are many extant documents that testify to the scientific and artistic legacy which al-Andalus left to the western world. Among the many scholarly disciplines that Arab culture introduced to Europe were cartography and surgery

•MANUSCRIPT COPIES *of the Koran from the Almoravid period, above.*

• THE ALBOLAFIA MILL, *really a water wheel, is situated just down-river from the Roman bridge. It dates from the XII century and is typ-* *ical of the hydraulic ingenuity of Andalucían Muslims. These great wheels were rotated by the current generated in deliberately constructed mill races, or weirs, and lifted the water with their paddles carrying earthenware containers, from whence it*

•THE MINARET OF ABD AR-RAHMAN III, *part of which still survives in the tower of Córdoba Cathedral*

was collected both for drinking and irrigation. Such systems were used widely throughout the Muslim world during the middle ages and are still to be found in use to this day. Here at Albolafia the water wheel is just one of a chain of four mills situated on a line of small islands between weirs stretching across the whole river. Today the area is a nature reserve just in front of the Great Mosque and is home to many interesting species of birds and animals.

THE CITY

Honeycomb capital.

According to both archaeological remains and extant chronicles, Córdoba's walls at the beginning of the XI century stretched for 22 kilometres, which means that the city was more extensive in the middle ages than it is today, at the beginning of the XXI century. The present-day historical city centre occupies no more than a few hectares on the banks of the river, much too small an area for what was in the X century the most powerful and prestigious city in the western world.

① **THE SYNAGOGUE.**

CALLE DE LOS JUDÍOS 10, 957 20 29 28.

This is one of only three mediaeval synagogues remaining in Spain. It was built in the heart of the Jewish quarter at the beginning of the XIV century. Its architecture is in the Mudéjar style and its stucco walls are covered in Hebrew inscriptions.

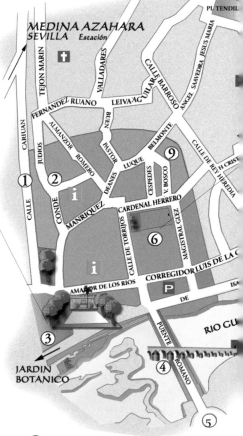

③ **THE CITADEL (ALCÁZAR) OF THE CHRISTIAN MONARCHS.**

CALLE DE LAS CABALLERIZAS REALES, s/n 957 42 01 51.

In 1328 King Alfonso XI ordered this fortress to be built close to the Great Mosque upon the remains of previous Roman and Arab structures, including a Muslim bath-house. It was to be called the citadel of the Christian Kings to distinguish it from the nearby castle which had been used by the Muslim caliphs. The Catholic Monarchs, Ferdinand and Isabel, lodged here at times during the long years of the Christian reconquest. It was later used by the Inquisition and then until 1951 as a prison. Nowadays its gardens and fountains lend it a much more agreeable aspect.able aspect.

⑧ **THE JULIO ROMERO DE TORRES MUSEUM.**
PLAZA DEL POTRO 1, 957 49 19 09.
This museum is dedicated to the work of the famous Córdoban painter, who managed to capture on his canvas the soul of Córdoba's womanhood of his day.

② **THE TAURINE MUSEUM.**
PLAZA DE MAIMÓNIDES s/n, 957 20 10 56.
This is Córdoba's most visited museum. I contains exhibits representing all aspects the bull fight together with memorabilia the great names of the bull ring in Córdoba, such as Lagartijo and Manolete

⑦ THE ARCHAEOLOGICAL MUSEUM.
Plaza de Jerónimo Páez, 7 957 47 40 11.
This museum is worth a visit not only for its exhibits but also for the Renaissance mansion which houses them. It has important local archaeological finds on show from the Roman, Visigothic and Muslim periods.

⑥ THE GREAT MOSQUE
The Great Mosque at Córdoba is one of the world's architectural wonders, the most striking example of Islamic art in the West and also one of lasting importance because of its technical and aesthetic innovations and its influence on the history of western art and architecture.

⑨ CALLEJA DE LAS FLORES
This narrow street, with its brilliantly contrasting geraniums hanging down against whitewashed walls, and the cathedral tower in the background, is perhaps the most representative of many such streets to be found in the old quarter of the city.

④ ROMAN BRIDGE
The Roman Bridge still rests upon its original Roman foundations, although having been the scene of numerous skirmishes and battles, and the victim of daily wear and tear, its superstructure has had to be rebuilt several times during its lifetime.

⑤ THE CALAHORRA TOWER
Standing on the south side of the river this tower was the key fortress guarding the mediaeval bridge. Today it houses the Museum of the Three Religions (Muslim, Jewish and Christian) and is designed to show Córdoba's prominence in learning and culture during the X century.

⑧ FINE ARTS MUSEUM.
PLAZA DEL POTRO, 1.957 47 33 45.
EThis museum is devoted mainly to artists of the Sevillian school, with paintings by Murillo, Zurburán and Valdés Leal, among others.

CORDOBA
IN FOCUS

• **THE GREAT MOS-
QUE AT CÓRDOBA.**
*Right: a view of the
prayer hall. The
twin colours, based
upon the combina-
tion of brick and
stone voussoirs,
alternating red and
white, creates an
illusion of space
with no defined
axis, static whilst at
the same time
dynamic, opening
in all directions at
once. Only 856 of
the original 1,013
columns remain,
the others having
been demolished
during Christian
reforms.*

EARLIER ARCHITECTURAL EXAMPLES.

After the first mosque at Medina the next to be built were those
at Kufa (638) and Amru (642), which already had brick-built
columns. Shortly after this the Umayyads, the true initiators of
Islamic architecture, raised the Dome of the Rock in Jerusalem.
But the mosques which began the architectural tradition in the
early years of the VIII century and shaped the direction of later
Islamic art were the Great Mosque at Damascus in Syria (also
known as the Umayyad Mosque), built in 707 (above: the
courtyard of the Great Mosque at Damascus) and al-Aksa in
Jerusalem, built in 710 (below). In all of these mosques the debt
to pre-Islamic Christian basilicas is clearly visible, with their
naves lined by arches supporting an upper solid stretch of wall
upon which a second tier of smaller, more graceful arches is set
to let in the light. This structural sequence can be seen quite
commonly in classical architecture. The decoration of the walls
also clearly falls within this classical tradition, with Roman-
Byzantine mosaics depicting other structures and gardens. This
was soon to disappear, however, and give way in the mosque at
Córdoba to what we recognise as typically Islamic designs,
based upon the repetition of geometric elements and highly
stylised vegetal designs framed by religious inscriptions.

• **ABOVE:** *the
minaret of the
mosque at Kairuan
(Tunis); below: a
view of the
mosque at al-Aksa
in Jerusalem.*

The influence of Syrian architectural design spread through
north Africa via Qariuan in Tunis and thence to Spain and
Córdoba, where eighty years later it would be given a fresh
impulse, which improved on many features of the original
mosques upon which it was modeled. Unlike the earlier
mosques, such as that in Damascus, where the dominating
theme of the architecture was strictly aligned, solidly defined
and imposingly high, the Great Mosque at Córdoba relies
on a new con-
cept of space,
hor-

izontal rather than imposingly vertical, static whilst at the same time dynamic, open in all directions. Another anomaly often pointed out is the orientation (qiblah) of the mihrab, which instead of facing Mecca (N112º from Córdoba) is orientated N150º, Various explanations have been put forward for this curiosity, some more

• MOSAICS.*In the Umayyad mosque (above) the mosaics clearly follow the late-Roman-*

curious than the curiosity itself, but the most likely is the entirely pragmatic one that the Muslims had already been using part of the old Church of St. Vincent for some time and when it was converted entirely into a mosque they saw no reason to start knocking down the whole structure to realign it with Mecca. Nevertheless, there have been suggestions that Abd ar-Rahman I orientated his mihrab towards where he arrived in Spain and in fact N150º from Córdoba aligns directly with the small coastal village of Almuñecar, where legend has it that he first landed on Spanish soil.

Byzantine tradition. The hues are predominantly golden upon green and blue backgrounds (left: mosaics from the mihrab at Córdoba.

• THE PRAYER HALL *of of the Great Mosque at Damascus, where an impression of height and illumination is achieved by arraying a second tier of lighter arches above the bulk of the columns of the lower arcade*

•GRABADO DE LA
MEZQUITA Y DEL PUENTE.
El lado sur de la Mezquita ocupa el centro del dibujo.

•GRABADO ROMÁN-
TICO DE LA
MEZQUITA.
Debajo vista de 180º desde la torre.

THE BUILDING OF THE MOSQUE

The following commentary is to be found in contemporary Arab chronicles: *"When the number of Muslims grew in al-Andalus and Córdoba was flourishing, and Arab princes settled there with their armies, the mosque became too small and they had to attach galleries to the walls, which caused a great nuisance to the people, who suffered a great deal because of the cramped space..."*. When the Arabs first conquered Córdoba they bought from the Christians half the Church of St. Vincent to use for their Friday prayers and thus the church was shared between Muslims and Christians. The rapid increase in the size of the Muslim population, however, soon rendered this arrangement unworkable and so in 784 Abd ar-Rahman bought the other half of the basilica to erect a mosque on the site. He paid the Christians well for their property and allowed them to build new churches in other parts of the town. Work on the mosque went apace as the Muslim masons took advantage of building materials already present in the basilica and plundered a lot more, such as columns with their bases and capitals and even shafts of timber, from the surrounding ruins of Roman and Visigothic mansions. The rulers who had ordered the construction participated very

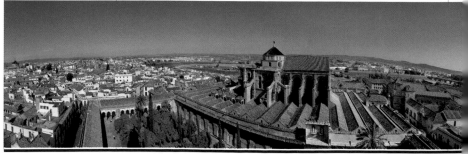

• **LEFT: THE GREAT MOSQUE AT DAMAS-CUS.** *Abd ar-Rahman I was highly influenced by the architectural traditions of the Near East, where he had spent much of his youth. Below: a Turkish miniature celebrating the call to prayer by*

closely in the building work and specialists on the subject have often wondered whether it might not have been Abd ar-Rahman himself who designed the mosque or whether he had architects brought from Syria. Whatever the truth of the matter, the underlying Syrian influence is quite obvious, on top of which local ingenuity contributed new creative architectural and decorative ideas that were to make the design of the mosque at Córdoba a model to be followed by others for centuries to come. The mosque was open for prayer in 785, just a year after the work began, although it was not finished by the time Abd ar-Rahman died in 788. It was left to his son Hishan I to put the finishing touches to the square minaret in the courtyard, which was completed in 793.

the first muezzin, who, by all accounts, was a negro called Bilal.

- **THE IMPOSITION** *of one row of arches upon another had its architectural precedents in Spain. The Roman aqueduct at Mérida, for example, combines superimposed masonry arches in which brick alternates with stone, just as in the voussoirs of the mosque in Córdoba.*

- **THE VI CENTURY CHURCH OF SAN JUAN** *de Baños is one of several Visigothic constructions in the Iberian peninsula that used the horseshoe arch long before the arrival of the Arabs in the Spanish peninsula*

- **THE STRUCTURE OF THE HORSE-SHOE ARCH,** *is based on the superimposition of arches the individual vertices of which shift in alignment as they descend in the vertical plane of the arch itself.*

The concept of the mosque (in Arabic mezquita, meaning "a place to prostrate oneself") originated at the house of the prophet Muhammad when he and his followers met for Friday prayer. It was an open yard in which some palm trunks supported a thatch of woven branches to protect the worshippers from

- **THE AQUEDUCT OF THE MIRACLES AT MÉRIDA.**

the heat of the sun. There was no tradition of permanent architecture among desert dwellers; it was the Umayyads who, under the influence of Greco-Roman tradition, raised the Dome of the Rock in Jerusalem in 687 and the Great Mosque at Damascus in 707. In Córdoba the need for a much wider space than that provided by a high basilica-like structure made a virtue of necessity and thus inspired brilliantly innovative architectural ideas.

The materials used to build many mosques in Spain at this time were plundered from nearby Roman and Visigothic ruins. In Córdoba the columns found round and about were not so tall as those used in Syrian mosques and could not provide the height required and so the creative genius of the unknown architect, probably inspired by the Roman Aqueduct of the Miracles at Mérida (see above)

decided to create first of all a horizontal line of imposts from which he "hung" the columns of various sizes, making them all the same height by adding extra sections beneath them to build up their bases or else sinking them into the ground if they were too tall. That is say, he evened out their irregularities from below rather than above. Upon the columns he placed the also plundered capitals and above these heavy cymas, or abacuses, in the shape of inverted tree trunks so as

• **A REMINDER OF HOME-LANDS.** *The forest of columns within the mosque must have reminded Arab worshippers of a grove of date palms, because for them the date palm was the quintessential symbol of their distant homeland, just like the mosaic that adorns the reliquary in the Umayyad mosque, which symbolises the fact that paradise is to be found in Damascus (see the illustration below).*

pilaster

abacus

line of imposts

PROJECTION AND VIEW OF THE FOREST OF COLUMNS. By superimposing two tiers of arches in the prayer hall Abd ar-Rahman's architect had arrived at an extraordinarily ingenious solu-tion to the problem of creating height and space inside the mosque despite the limited height of the pillars he had available. Upon the capital of each column he placed a heavy abacus and upon this a thick pilaster which acts as an elongation of the column below and supports the upper tier of arches and the weight of the roof.

to gain volume while ascending. On top sit even wider pilasters, their salient shafts adorned with newly crafted mouldings designed in Córdoba. Finally, on top of the pilasters he installed the springings for the upper tier of semi-circular arches, which were also wider than the pilasters themselves, all of which supported the roof. But this elegant structure, wider at the top than at the bottom, was innately unstable and in danger of collapse and so the architect came up with the ingenious solution that makes the Córdoba mosque so special: he fitted in a lower tier of horse-shoe arches resting upon the abacuses and abutting crosswise with the width of the pilasters supporting the upper arches, thus acting as tie beams to brace the whole structure firmly togeth-er. In this way he was able to leave the arches completely open and give the mosque a sensation of space and light.

• SPACE IN THE MOSQUE.

Stierlin remarks that, Never before had such wide internal spaces been conceived of by such simple means as columns supporting relatively small arches. Neither the hypostyle rooms in the Pharaonic temples at Karnak and Luxor nor Roman basilicas, nor Constantinian churches could compare with these delicate spaces so full of air and light. Probably only the largest of the Roman and Byzantine cisterns had given rise to schemes such as this

Another innovation compared to the Umayyad Mosque at Damascus is that the aisles run towards the qiblah rather than parallel to it. The central aisle, which leads to the mihrab, is wider, in the style of a church nave, and gives the impression of an overall convergence towards the mihrab but without disrupting the uniformity of the overall space of the mosque.

Left: part of the first extension to the mosque ordered by Abd ar-Rahman II in 833, when eleven more naves were added running in the direction of the qiblah. Building materials pillaged from other sites were again used in the construction, although seventeen of the new capitals were carved by Córdoban stonemasons. The columns stand without bases and are all smooth except for two, which have vertical fluting, and one with a spiral design.

THE EXTENSION OF THE MOSQUE.

Although the Great Mosque was built over a period of more than 200 years, during which time modifications were constantly being made to it, the original basic structure was only added to but never radically altered, perhaps to some degree in respect to its builder, but above all because it already comprised all the elements and technical and aesthetic discoveries common to perfect works of art. Hishan I (788-796) finished off the work begun by his father Abd a Rahman I by building the first minaret. Forty years later Abd ar-Rahman II (822-852) made the first extension to the prayer hall (833), adding eight new aisles, half of which are now lost beneath the Christian cathedral. During this building phase, which took fifteen years to complete, old columns were also used from other ruined buildings. These were set directly into the floor without base but any missing capitals (seventeen in all) were replaced by new ones carved in Córdoban workshops. A hundred years after that, in 951, the caliph Abd ar-Rahman III built a new minaret 48 metres high, of which only 22 metres survive today incorporated into the cathedral tower. The influence of this minaret is to be seen reflected in all the new minarets built thereafter throughout the western Islamic world. On widening the courtyard Abd ar-Rahman had also to restructure it entirely, extending it 60 metres farther to the north. He also surrounded its three hitherto open sides with the riwat, a six-metre-wide arcaded gallery in which pillars alternate with columns. But it was his son al Hakam II, the pious, learned prince, who on his father's behalf had been supervising the work on the royal city of Madinat az-Zahra, who, on the day after ascending to the throne, decided that the mosque was once more too small to satisfy the demands of an ever growing population and set out to extend it again. He demolished the qiblah wall and moved it 12 aisles farther to the south, as far in fact as the river would allow, thus making the prayer hall 104 metres long. He erected the maqsura, a screen to form a sanctuary before the mihrab, and converted the mihrab itself into the most refined example of the whole mosque. The final extension to the mosque was made twenty-four years later by the usurper general Abu Amir Muhammad al-Mansur, who widened it eastwards by eight naves.

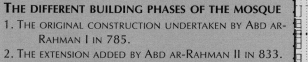

THE DIFFERENT BUILDING PHASES OF THE MOSQUE

1. THE ORIGINAL CONSTRUCTION UNDERTAKEN BY ABD AR-
   RAHMAN I IN 785.
2. THE EXTENSION ADDED BY ABD AR-RAHMAN II IN 833.
3. ADDITIONS MADE BY ABD AR-RAHMAN III IN 945.
4. THE MAQSURA AND NEW MIHRAB BUILT BY AL-HAKAN II
   IN 961.
5. FINAL EXTENSIONS ADDED BY AL-MANSUR IN 987.
   A) THE COURT OF THE ORANGE TREES.
   B) THE MINARET.

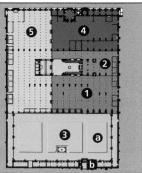

• SECTIONS OF THE ROOFING AS DEDUCED BY M. NIETO CUMPLIDO. *The roof was constructed of wooden beams and rafters, which were then hidden by a sumptuous ceiling decorated with gold and multi-coloured motifs.*

• THE FLOOR OF THE MOSQUE *was made of argamasa, a compact, red-dish mixture of slaked lime and sand, which would then have been covered in mats and carpets just as today in the majority of mosques.*

25

• THE INTERIOR OF THE MOSQUE

The interior of the communal prayer hall of the Great Mosque in Córdoba, gives the visitor the sensation of entering into a different world from that which he has just left outside, a world where space expands in all directions and the translucent arches suspended above his head like weightless palms are endlessly interwoven and stretch away to eternity. *The pillars rise vertically above the capitals like branches striving upward towards the light. The red and white voussoirs of the arches emphasise the sensation of space repeating itself and expanding towards the unreachably far horizon.* (A. Muñoz Molina).

For the Muslim worshipper the perfectly parallel symmetry between the floor and the ceiling flow in unison towards a limitless infinity, a mystical void, the bare simplicity of his personal relationship with God.

The multi-lobular arches (left), which are typical of Syrian Abbasid architecture, are in fact the strongest elements in the structure. They are subtly interwoven to absorb the many different angles of thrust exerted upon them whilst at the same time giving the impression of lightness and delicacy.

• XVIII CENTURY
ENGRAVING BY
GIRAULT DE PRANGEY

AL-HAKAM II. THE MAQSURAH AND THE MIHRAB.

Al-Hakam II did not pillage his building materials from elsewhere but had columns and capitals hewn in his own workshops. The lack of light and insufficient ventilation in the mosque prompted him to construct four lanterns in the roof and once again necessity gave rise to an ingenious solution. The stronger supports required for the extra weight seem to be made more graceful by the open spaces they create as they cross the multi-lobular arches (this page). But this is deceptive as they are interlaced by elegant ribs which bind in a central knot, thus absorbing the

• THE STRUCTURE OF THE ARCHES. *The lower tier of multi-lobular arches are overlapped by the upper ones, thus sharing the weight where they intersect and directing the final downward thrust into the columns. The interweaving of a multitude of arches indicates at one and the same time the physical screen of maqsurah, whilst the richness of its adornment emphasises the nobility of the sanctuary reserved for the caliph before the mihrab.*

many counterthrusts and increasing the overall distribution of the weight. Above this stone latticework rises the ribbed cupola, which seems to float on its octagonal base of fine ribbing, arched into two squares intersecting at an angle of 45°. This ribbed vault, serving as a soffit to centre the dome, is divided into small segments and was thus much easier to vault over, the vaulting here being made of stone and not brick as it tended to be in Persia some hundred years later (see opposite page).

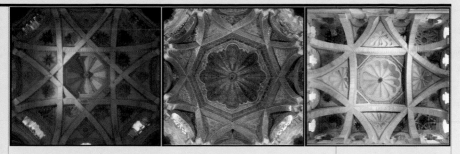

THE SANCTUARY BEHIND THE MAQSURAH

It is in this small area of the mosque, reserved for the caliph's private prayer, where the art of the Córdoban caliphate can be seen to have reached maturity and where eastern and western traditions combine most successfully. According to Enrique Pareja, the Arabs inherited the horseshoe arch and the agave capital from Hispano-Visigothic architecture and figurative representation from Byzantine architecture. From their Abbasid rivals they borrowed the multi-lobular arch and the stylisation of natural shapes.

- **IN 961 AL-HAKAN** *built two ribbed domes on either side of the original main dome (see illustration). It is unlikely that ribbed cupolas had their origin in earlier buildings in the Near East; it seems more probable that they were the invention of the Spanish caliphate and may also have gone on to inspire some of the ideas to be seen in Gothic architecture.*

•PROYECCIÓN LONGITUDINAL

What was genuinely Umayyad in origin seems to have been the idea of the transept, the rectangular minaret, and above all the rounded cupola unsupported by ribbing. The Córdoban contribution to caliphal architecture was the ribbed vault, the ataurique vegetal motifs and the honeycombed marble capitals. (Various types of these cupolas are depicted

- **CROSS SECTION OF THE MAQSURAH PRECINCT** *(left). The first three bays of the central nave constitute the approach to the oratory of al-Hakan II. In this way the area, or sanctuary, before the mihrab remains cut off from the rest of the prayer hall by this enormous masonry jalousie, the maqsurah.*

On the double page overleaf, a view of the main cupola from beneath.

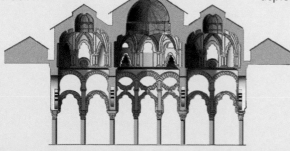

- **THE SANCTUARY BEHIND THE MAQSURAH IN AN ORIGINAL PLATE BY C. EWERT.**

Inside the mosque the prayer hall achieves its height and airiness through two tiers of arches. In the confines behind the maqsurah, however, lanterns needed to be built into the roof to illuminate the area just before the mihrab.

AL-HAKAN II. THE MAQSURAH AND THE MIHRAB

•AN ARCH BESIDE THE MIHRAB.

The mihrab as such first appeared in the mosque at Medina when it was rebuilt by the Umayyads but it was in Córdoba that it became most refined and was for the first time incorporated as a niche into the far wall of the prayer hall, indicating the qiblah, or direction towards Mecca. The concept of a niche may have owed its inspiration to the Christian apse or the niche in Roman households where their divinities were displayed. But in the Córdoban mosque what had originally been just a groove cut in the wall to mark the qiblah became an octagonal niche with a ceiling sculpted from a single block of white marble into the shape of a scallop shell, the symbol of life, the word of God, beneath which, to celebrate special occasions, a copy of the Koran written out in the hand of Oman himself was placed. Although everywhere is recognised as being sacred and apt for prayer, "Turn wherever you will and you will find the face of God" the mihrab became the focus for the faithful to prostrate themselves before their God, a symbolic doorway leading to heaven where they directed their prayers, a symbol of the absolute, an affirmation of the divine within this world. What had originated as a simple reference point to the qiblah became in the Great Mosque at Córdoba a focus of enormous religious significance. For this reason the mihrab had to be the most sumptuously adorned place in the mosque to attract the eyes of the worshippers. (On the preceding page, a view of the mihrab)

•AL-HAKAM II was one of the most learned men of his day. He had a library of 400,000 books containing the whole of human knowledge of that time.

•LEFT: The chapel at Villaviciosa in an XVIII century engraving by Girault de Prangey.

INSCRIPCIONES EN CARACTERES CÚFICOS
*Alusivas a suras coránicas que deco-
ran la puerta de entrada al Mihrab.*

THE MIHRAB.

When he was heir to the throne al-Hakan, the learned and extremely pious prince, had overseen the building work on the royal city of Madinat az-Zahra and so it is not surprising that when he ascended the throne his very first royal command was to begin forthwith on the most important reforms that the mosque had ever seen and it is equally certain that his personal intervention in its design had a decisive influence on the growth in maturity of Córdoban art. He had no hesitation in asking the Christian emperor Nicephorus Phocas for advice In the adornment of the mihrab, just as the first of the Umayyads had turned to Christendom for help in Damascus 250 years before. Whilst Charlemagne sided with he Abbasids, the Córdoban Umayyads had come to an understanding with the Christian empire in the east. From this alliance the emir received 320 quintales nearly 15 tonnes) of brightly coloured glassware, some of it covered in gold leaf, together with the services of a master builder to teach the Córdoban artisans the Byzantine technique of mosaic decoration. In the words of Gómez Moreno, We have to go back to Santa Sofia to find anything comparable to the exquisite elegance of this mihrab.

• **THE FAÇADE OF THE MIHRAB.**
The intentions of the first architect were completely respected in all the later extensions to the mosque, as can be seen in the use of his scheme to frame the horseshoe arch above the outer door in a closed spandrel (855). Above, to the right: St Stephen's doorway. This design was copied in the façade of the mihrab (above left), to which Umayyad

decoration was added in the shape of Byzantine marble and tiling. Also woven into the design were delicately contrived ribbonwork and ataurique motifs of oriental origin, belonging to the so-called second style, which, together with intricate honeycombing in the capitals, became the hallmarks of this apotheosis of Spanish caliphal architecture.

• THE DECORATION OF THE ARCH BEFORE THE MIHRAB. *The twin red and white colouring of the voussoirs of the arches which meets the eye upon entering the mosque was translated some centuries later on this arch above the entrance to the mihrab into a fantastic interplay of ataurique designs upon backgrounds of blue, red and gold (left), creating a symmetrical repetition of unidentifiable floral motifs reminiscent of far-off Damascus.*

The date when the line of imposts was finished is inscribed in tiny red Kufic characters upon a gold background as being 965. Inscriptions from the Koran stand out clearly against blue and gold backgrounds around the spandrel of the arch.

The stylised vegetal designs on the blind arches within the mihrab and the use of colour are of rare and delicate simplicity.

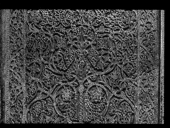

• DECORATIVE FEATURES. *The elaborate floral motifs used in Spanish-Umayyad decoration include leaves and calices, rosettes, palm sprays, clover leaves, pineapples and bunches of grapes. These individual elements are also intricately decorated within themselves and their edges are often jagged or feathered into leaf-like designs.*

A fragment of the tree of life, originally a Syro-Persian concept, incised using the so-called "soft-chisel" technique because of the delicacy of its carving.

• THE CUPOLA OF THE MIHRAB. *The interior of the mihrab is an octagonal recess crowned by a single white marble dome sculpted into the form of a shell, which symbolises the word of the Koran and is thus related to ancient belief which identified the shell as the symbol of the source of* life. Henceforth it became customary to decorate the mihrab with a scallop shell, which had the added advantage of helping to amplify the voice of the imam when leading communal prayer.

The scallop is also a symbol associated with the Virgin Mary and the Immaculate Conception, the generator of life, and thus Christians are born to a life of grace via baptism by water poured from the shell. It is also to be found in many other cultures because of its connotations with water, the life-giver, and sometimes represents the female sexual organ..

• The Arab geographer al-Idrisi wrote in the XII century, Among all the Muslim mosques it

al-Mansur's extension

Abu Amir al-Mansur began his career as a government functionary in Algeciras, but by intrigue and betrayal in equal measure managed to climb to the highest ranks of power, and finally in 981 sequestered power from the weak caliph Hishan II and imposed his own absolute rule. Due once more to the steady increase in Córdoba's population and his own desire to ingratiate himself with the religious leaders who questioned the legality of his rule and his tendencies to nepotism and clientage in government, al-Mansur decided to make further extensions to the Great Mosque.

has no equal, for the beauty of its architecture and its great size and also for its adornments.

Because of the proximity of the river to the south his architects were obliged to add on the eight new naves eastwards, which meant a displacement of the whole building with regard to the central aisle, the mihrab and the minaret, although the final shape of the building was left more regular than it had been.

Where the new building work was tagged onto the old can be discerned at a glance. This final extension to the mosque lacks any innovatory ideas and most of its architectural features, such as the columns and their capitals and the arches with their limestone voussoirs, picked out in red and white, are almost bureaucratic in their uniform obedience to traditional design. The arches are fairly reduced in size in an attempt to harmonise the new work with those already in place. During repairs to the roof in the XVIII century lunettes

• **PANORAMIC VIEW OF THE MOSQUE.**

• **THE MILITARY LEADER ABU AMIR AL-MANSUR,** *originally regent to the caliph Hisham II, assumed total power in 981 after returning from a victorious campaign spreading terror amongst the Christians.*

were opened to give more light to this new extension and at the easternmost end the original coffered ceiling was replaced with a barrel vault. Seven new doors were also opened in the eastern wall, which, despite their elaborate decoration, betray a general decadence of artistic talent.

SCULPTURE.

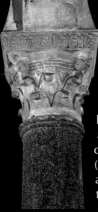

The original mosque contained almost 150 capitals pillaged from other Visigothic and Roman monuments and so they represent a multitude of styles from the preceding centuries. The craftsmanship in them is also fairly disparate, some belonging to very elaborate classical Corinthian and late-Roman periods whilst other Visigothic ones were quite simply and roughly hewn, although often full of ingenious elegance: these are known as agave capitals (left), which are often composite, showing a combination of a basic Corinthian form with stylised Ionic volutes (below left). During the first extension process in the IX century, although some pre-Islamic capitals were also brought in, seventeen new ones, copied from those already in place for conformity's sake, were moulded in Córdoban workshops. Their abacuses are Christian-Visigothic in style and are decorated with typical geometric shapes and vine leaves among which appear Christian crosses.

Right: the Visigothic altar; its upper section is missing and the horizontal arms of the Christian cross carved in relief on its side have been chipped off. Its decoration is typically Visigothic with friezes of simple repetitious geometric motifs. It is now forms part of a small display of archaeological finds within the mosque itself.

It can often be seen that because the capitals have been taken from other buildings they are smaller in diameter than the column beneath them.

Left: a caliphal column base moulded in the same style as the honeycomb capitals.

To the left is a translucent, white-marble Roman column, remarkable here because of its vertically fluted shaft.

According to Gómez Moreno the collection of capitals used in the Great Mosque at Córdoba makes it the ideal place to study the evolution of the classical capital and its transformation at the hands of the Visigoths; a veritable living museum of architectural marvels that would not have survived had they not been re-used in this way.

The X century capital, used frequently in Madinat az-Zahra, was derived from the Corinthian capital. The stylised acanthus leaves sprouting from the abacus are filled with perforations, giving rise to the so-called "honeycomb" capital, which continued to evolve until the end of the Nasrid dynasty in Granada in the XV century.

To the right are two of the four columns of black marble and red pudding stone from the Sierra de Cabra, used in the first extension and then re-used by al-Hakan II in the final mihrab.

To the left is a view of one of the aisles belonging to the final extension carried out by al-Mansur, in which the original schemes are repeated but which also illustrates the depth and lucidity achieved with a felicitous combination of arches.

• **THE INTERIOR OF A GALLERY AROUND THE COURT OF THE ORANGE TREES.**

The sahn, or courtyard, was surrounded by roofed galleries, as are those of most of the great mosques throughout the world, except for the side communicating with the prayer hall, which can be reached via nineteen arcaded aisles. In a very few mosques, such as the Umayyad Mosque in Damascus, this side is also closed leaving the windows opened in the quiblah wall to allow light into the naves. In the majority, however, as in Córdoba, a diffuse northern light spills in from the courtyard and plays among the forest of pillars from ground level. No other contemporary mosque had such a large prayer hall as that at Córdoba and the distance to the mihrab also made it essential to build lanterns in the roof.

It is difficult from the outside to discern the variety of elements which make up the building as a whole and their relative asymmetry, due to al-Mansur's having to add his eight naves to the east rather than towards the river, make the internal layout of the mosque somewhat unusual.

THE COURTYARD OF THE ORANGE TREES

The courtyard is fundamental to any mosque and is normally the place where the fountain for ritual ablution is to be found. In Córdoba the courtyard was originally surrounded by a wall (left) but Abd ar-Rahman III built arcades

in which much of the daily activity of the mosque took place. The mosque, apart from being a place of prayer was, and indeed still is, equivalent to the town square in western tradition, a place to meet and to talk or just to watch life go by. These porticoes were witness to much of the hustle and bustle of the daily round of city life.

Above left is a reconstruction of the first mosque and to the right an old postcard of the courtyard photographed before the arcades were discovered in the last century.

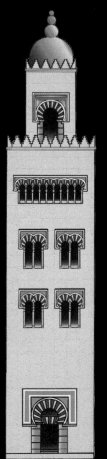

•A WINDOW IN THE MINARET
on each side, according to Félix Hernández, who has studied the minaret in detail. Part of it survives today incorporated into the tower.

THE MINARET.
The word alminar, or minaret, means in Arabic "the place of light", the place from whence is promulgated the Word which will illuminate the soul as the light dispels the darkness. There has been much speculation about the second minaret erected by Abd ar-Rahman III; some scholars claim that it was crowned by three golden spheres, others say five. What is sure is that it was 47.5 metres high. Félix Hernández left us his drawings, which served as a model for the infographic reproduction on the left. Its shape and structure were reproduced in many later minarets, including those at Marrakech, Rabat and Sevilla (the present-day Giralda), together with other contemporary ones which today are church towers.

•THE COURTYARD OF THE ORANGE TREES.
This is the sahn of the mosque, enclosed on three sides from the middle of the X century. Its name derives from the fact that the Christian conquerors planted orange trees here, although in Muslim times there had been other types of trees there.there.

• ABOVE: VIEW OF THE DOOR OF PARDONS

•THE TOWER
In 1593 Hernán Ruiz the younger built a second storey onto the minaret to accommodate the bells and the clock but later because of repeated earth tremors it was thought advisable to construct an outer strengthening wall, concealing what was left of the original minaret, and that is what we see today. Later still, a third storey was added on top of which stands the Archangel Raphael, guardian angel of the city of Córdoba. The last repairs were finished in 1763 and show the clear influence of the Sevillian late-Renaissance architect Sebastián Herrera.

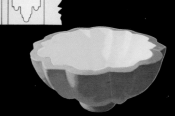

•THE MARBLE BOWL FOR WASHING BEFORE PRAYER
Such a facility is essential in or beside all mosques to allow the faithful to wash before prayer. The bowl in the Courtyard of the Orange Trees was originally filled from a well beneath it but al-Hakan II built an aqueduct to bring water from the mountains behind the city to fill an aljibe, or cistern. Al-Mansur then dug an even bigger cistern, capable of holding some 600,000 litres of water.

● BELOW: THE BASIC STRUCTURE OF ST. STEPHEN'S DOORWAY *(855) follows the original architect's design but later decorative additions have been made in a mixture of both Visigothic and Umayyad styles. The modillions above the doorway and the stepped-pyramid crenellation are Córdoban*

innovations which were later copied extensively in many other places.

THE ARCHITECTURE OF THE FAÇADE.

The doorways into the original mosque were notable for their harmony of design but of the four doorways in each side of the first building only one remains, that of St. Stephen (San Estebán or San Sebastián) in the western wall. It is a classic example of the typical Córdobam tripartite, buttressed doorway and with its rich architectural adornment and monumental mien is not only an exceptional work of art but also completely original in design. There is nothing similar to

it in contemporary architecture and according to Professor Torres Balbas we need to go back to late-Roman structures such as Diocletian's Porta Aurea in Split (Dalmatia) to find anything resembling this architectural achievement.

The four outer walls encompass an area of some 22,400 square metres and contain twelve doorways. Those in the western wall, introduced during the reform of al-Hakan II, follow the general tripartite composition of St. Stephen's doorway, with their arches elegantly interlaced, the simple clean lines of the projecting borders around the spandrels and the great variety in decorative motifs. The upper sections of the structure on both sides of the doorway proper

• DECORATION OF THE EXTERIOR WINDOWS. *The motifs are a symmetrical repetition of geometric shapes extended towards infinity by multiplying, dividing and rotating them until they become a metaphor of eternity*

• A MARBLE JALOUSIE *to one side of St. Stephen's doorway. This is the oldest surviving exterior decoration in the mosque*

are composed of overlapping horseshoe arches and the windows are composite, or multilobular, arches. The ataurique designs are very similar to those adorning the mihrab

• **INTERLACED ARCHES.** *Above the doors themselves there are richly decorated friezes, with interlaced arches supported upon small marble columns. Chiselled into the stone wall are alternating designs of vine leaves and swastikas crosses. The perforated capitals are reminiscent of Byzantine art; they support strong imposts which in turn absorb the downward thrust of the overhanging arches. Right: details of the doorways of al-Hakan II and St. Michael.*

and the stone and brickwork marquetry of the pavement resembles that found in the royal city of Madinat az-Zahra. The interwoven jalousies reveal the Byzantine influence that shaped the basic elements of this style of Córdoban doorway, although they were crassly restored at the beginning of the XX century and substantial changes were made

to the upper parts of the doorways by Professor Velásquez Bosco, with no real reference being made to the original design, and unnecessary apocryphal introductions were inserted into the epigraphic texts.

The main doorway, the "Door of Pardons", is in the northern façade and is clearly Almohad in style. Many of the

• **ORNAMENTATION.** *The doors along the side walls of the mosque are very characteristic in their decoration: the arches slightly projecting with heavy keystones, framing multi-lobular, windows filled in with marble. Above: St. Michael's Doorway and right: the Doorway of al-Hakan II.*

doorways in the western wall have been subject to considerable alteration since the XVI century, easily discernible by the Christian details incorporated into the additions, particularly the door of St. Stephen, already described above, and that of al-Hakan II.

There was also a small doorway close to the river that gave onto a passage-

•A RECONSTRUCTION OF THE SABAT DOORWAY BUILT BY AL-HAKAN, *according to the scheme proposed by L. Golvin, based upon contemporary accounts that speak of a door leading to a walkway above street level supported upon five arches and divided into five separate "rooms" along its length.*

•THE EASTERN FAÇADE, BUILT BY AL-MANSUR.

● THE EASTERN
FAÇADE, *built by al-
Mansur. To the
right are the six
doors which were
over-restored by
Velázquez Bosco
at the beginning of
the XX century.*

● RIGHT: VIEW OF
THE DOOR OF
PARDONS

●AN INSCRIPTION BY
ABD AR-RAHMAN III
*beside the Arch of
Blessings.*

way crossing over a system of arches connecting the mosque to the caliphal citadel, the alcázar. According to the contemporary writer Ibn Hayyan, there was a raised walkway known as the *sabat*, which resembled a covered bridge supported by one or more arches, spanning the gap (nowadays Torrijos street) between the two buildings. When al-Hakan II extended the mosque he did away with this original passageway but built himself a new one which existed until 1622 when it was demolished during restoration work on the bishop's palace.

The whole of the original eastern façade was knocked down by al-Mansur, including some of the doorways made during al-Hakan's reforms 120 years before. Nonetheless,

sufficient remains still exist of one of al-Hakan's doorways, now inside the mosque and known as the "Chocolate Gate", to appreciate the beauty of its *ataurique* designs and marquetry. Although al-

Mansur did not skimp on materials in his extension to the mosque he confined himself to copying the earlier designs both on the inside and in the six gateways which he modelled on those of al-Hakan before him, but of much mean-

er design. His only slight innovation in the doorways was in the incorporation of twin horseshoe arches, although this design had first been seen in the minaret of Abd ar-Rahman seventy years earlier.

• **A RECONSTRUCTION** *of the western façade of the mosque before its restoration at the beginning of the XX century by Professor Velásquez Bosco..*

• **XVIII CENTURY ENGRAVINGS** *by Girault de Prangey. Left: the western façade and details of some of the doorways before their restoration.*

• LEFT: THE **DOORWAY OF THE HOLY GHOST,** *which was totally restored by Velásquez Bosco.*

CÓRDOBA CATHEDRAL

After the reconquest in 1236 and the subsequent christianisation of the Great Mosque no immediate alterations were made to the building itself. It was not until nearly 200 years later, in 1523, that Bishop Alonso Manrique obtained permission from his uncle the Emperor Charles V to build a cathedral inside the mosque. Afterwards the emperor regretted his decision when on a visit to the city during his honeymoon in 1526 he saw what his avuncular benevolence had led to. But it was too late to stop the work, which went on for nearly a hundred years under the supervision of Hernán Ruiz the elder and then Hernan Ruiz the younger and Juan de Ochoa. The building was not in fact finished until 1766 and architectural tastes and concepts had obviously changed during those 250 years. The Hernan Ruízs, father, son and grandson, watched over

•THE CUPOLA.
View of the oval cupola in the late-Gothic transept, in the style of Herrera.

•*Left: page from a* BOOK OF BALLADS *of Alfonso X, the Wise. Above, a page from a choral missal.*

• AN ENGRAVING OF THE ROYAL CHAPEL *and a view of the Christian Cathedral within the Great Mosque in the photograph. Below: a lion's head belonging to one of the pulpits carved by Miguel Verdiguier.*

• MUDÉJAR CUPOLA *and multi-lobular arch in the Royal Chapel.*

the transition from the late-Renaissance to the Plateresque and then to the most elaborate Spanish Baroque, the Churrigueresque.

The main chapel of the cathedral is a prime example of this mixture: the arches in the form of the Roman cross are Gothic whilst the vaults over the central nave and the transept owe their style to

Herrera. The altar screen dates from 1618 and is the work of the Jesuit master craftsman Alonso Matías. It is carved from red marble and jasper from the Córdoban quarries of Carcabuey and Cabra, which frame the paintings of Palomino. Worthy of attention are the two pulpits by Verdiguier, carved in mahogany and supported by symbols of the four evangelists, each sculpted in differently coloured

stone (left: the lion of St. Mark in red jasper). But most outstanding of all is the choir, carved in mahogany from the West Indies by Pedro Duque Cornejo in the middle of the XVIII century. In a masterly display of craftsmanship he includes a whole range of religious themes ranging from biblical scebnes to images of Córdoban martyrs. The choir stalls are fairly uniform except for the magnificent bishop's throne in which the whole canon of Baroque rhetoric is displayed to its full effect and symbolism: the Ascent of our Lord among the apostles, crowned by the Archangel Raphael, guardian angel of Córdoba, is surrounded by St. Theresa and St. Mary Magdalene, whose exemplary lives exert great doctrinal authority (left). The cathedral also contains more than fifty chapels, most of them occupying recesses in the walls, among which the Chapel of Cardinal Salazar, also known as the Chapel of St. Theresa, is noteworthy because of its splendid sculpture of St. Theresa, carved by José de Mora. Apart from being the sacristy it is also the chapter house, a typically octagonal Baroque structure, decorated by Hurtado Izquierdo, another of the last great masters of the Baroque along with Duque Cornejo and Palomino, who painted many of the portraits in the cathedral. Beside the chapter house is the treasury; its most valuable item is the early-XVI-century Gothic-style reliquary belonging to Enrique Arfe, measuring 2.63 metres and weighing more than 200 kilos.

CORDOBA

IN FOCUS

CORDOBA'S DOMESTIC COURTYARDSTHE JEWISH QUARTER OTHER POINTS OF INTEREST MUSEUMS

CÓRDOBA'S DOMESTIC COURTYARDS

●**THE FESTIVAL OF THE COURTYARDS** *and the springtime crosses. On 3 May Córdoba celebrates the festival of the cross when the whole city is filled with set pieces of crosses garlanded with flowers and a multitude of other traditional adornments. A week later there is a festival for individual courtyards, the best decorated receiving a considerable prize. Shortly afterwards is the festival of Nuestra Señora de la Salud.*

The *megaron* in ancient Greece and the *atrium* in Rome were open courtyards within the private house, often serving as the reception centre or business area for a patrician citizen. Family life would have gone on around these courtyards. The Arabs adopted the same concept, their dwellings opening onto an interior courtyard which did not usually enjoy the same splendid façades as the outside of the house.

●**THE TYPICAL DECORATION OF A CÓRDOBAN COURTYARD.**
The most important elements were the spring or well and the surrounding plants, but over the centuries the courtyard developed and became more ornate with elegant wrought-iron grilles and lamps, ceramic tiling and, above all, pots of flowers.

•**SPRINGS AND FOUNTAINS.** *The spring in a courtyard offers an oasis of freshness in the torrid heat of the Córdoban summer and without doubt the gentle murmur of flowing water is the sweetest of melodies in the baking silence of an August afternoon.*

What used to be an intimate space in family life has come over time to be the centre of social life among Córdoban neighbours. The potted plant, originally an idea conceived by desert nomads so as to be able to carry with them a small piece of living nature (those same nomadic Berbers who conquered and inhabited Córdoba in the VIII century), became the centrepiece of domestic decoration, beneath the shade of the inevitable grape vine or fruit tree overhanging the courtyard

•**CÓRDOBAN COURTYARDS**, *direct descendants of caliphal courtyards, share their design of shady arched porticoes, which alleviate the heat of summer and also capture the warmth of the winter sun.*

●**COLOUR.**
The whitewash on the walls of the houses is traditional to southern Spain. Zealously renewed every year, its main purpose used to be to disinfect the houses and also to reflect the fierce heat of the summer sun.

The courtyard in Córdoba has become a symbol of pride to the city but has of course undergone changes during its history. Once it was a strictly private part of an equally private

house, jealously guarded in narrow streets and closed off to the curious by iron gates and grilles. Today their owners are quite willing to show them to respectful visitors.

●**XIV** CENTURY SYNA-GOGUE. *One of the three mediaeval synagogues to have survived in Spain. Below: the seven-branched menorah.*

●**Maimónides**. *A great Spanish-Jewish philosopher, scientist and physician, was forced to flee with his family from persecution in Spain under the fanatical Almohads to Fez in north Africa and thence to Egypt, where he became personal physician to the sultan Saladin.*

THE JEWISH QUARTER

There are records dating from the third century A.D. testifying to Jewish settlements in the Iberian peninsula, of the persecution that they suffered under the Visigoths and of their alliances with the Muslims after the Arab conquest. But it was in the X century that they began to play an important role in Spanish Muslim society in the organisation of the caliph's rule, as administrators, doctors, businessmen and functionaries. al-Hakan II was in this respect a very tolerant ruler and was known as the lord of the three religions.

In Córdoba, as in the majority of medieval cities, the Jews tended to live in their own neighbourhoods, apart from the rest of the towns-people. The Jewish quarter must have been quite extensive and considerably important, close as it was to the wall surrounding the royal apartments and to the centre of administrative power. What remains today of the Jewish quarter, despite being considerably reduced in size, is little changed from how it must have been in the days of the caliphate: a maze of narrow, winding whitewashed streets, which lead into shady alleyways with glimpses of deliciously cool courtyards, or suddenly into peaceful, tree-lined squares, a delight for visitors and residents alike.

• **THE SYNAGOGUE.** The original synagogue is to be found in *calle Judios* (the street of the Jews) and is entered via a small courtyard and a narthex below the women's gallery. It was built in 1315 during the reign of the Christian king Alfonso XI in the Mudéjar style and decorated with stucco adornments which follow clearly in the tradition of Nasrid architecture in Granada. Within the heart of this thriving community one of

the greatest Jewish theologians and philosophers of all time was born and educated. The writings of Moses ben Maimon (1135-1204) more widely known as Maimónides, were prolific and covered a vast range of subjects. Before the age of 33 he had summarised the teachings of Judaism in a creed of Thirteen Articles of Faith. His *magnum opus*, however, is undoubtedly his commentary on the Torah, *Mishne Torah*, in which he systemises all of Jewish law and doctrine.

• **DETAILS OF THE XIV CENTURY SYNAGOGUE** *in The inscriptions above the Mudéjar ataurique motifs show that the Jews never developed an art form proper to themselves but simply adapted the styles of the time to their own needs.*

• *Above:* PUBLIC BATHS *from caliphal times in calle Velázquez Bosco. Below:* THE CHURCH OF ST. BARTHOLOMEW.

OTHER POINTS OF INTEREST

One of the most attractive features of Córdoba is the way in which a visitor can allow himself to be lead by his instincts and be surprised at every turning by hidden corners, courtyards and little squares, wander through the narrow, twisting alleyways surrounding the mosque, streets which from Moorish times have changed their route according to the needs of the houses and their residents rather than imposing their will on the whole shape of the city, as we can see in the streets and avenues of some modern cities. Muñoz Molina comments that its streets seem to be designed especially for visitors who are in no hurry, and their twists and turns increase the pleasure of strolling and observing.... *La calleja de las Flores* (Blossom Lane, below) typifies the synthesis of perfumes and colours in these streets, and with the cathedral tower emerging from a background of geraniums hanging down from the wrought-iron balconies is a classic example of their beauty. The XVI century theatre was in the adjacent *calle Comedias.*

• DETAIL OF THE SHIELD IN THE PLAZA DE LAS FLORES (BLOSSOM SQUARE).

• **THE ROMAN BRIDGE.**
The superstructure of the Roman bridge has been rebuilt several times during its long life but it still sits upon its original Roman foundations. In 1651, after the plague had ravaged the city, its townspeople erected a statue of their guardian angel, the Archangel Raphael, in the town centre.

Also nearby are the streets of San Fernando (popularly known as La Feria), an avenue of orange trees with its Baroque fountain, and the Arco del Portillo, an archway which opens onto calle Cabezas. At the southern end of the long Roman bridge, over which ran the Via Augusta, in the Campo de la Verdad, stands the Calahorra Tower, built by Alfonso XI upon the remains of an old Arab fortress almost a century after the reconquest. Enrique II, the first of the Trastamara dynasty, added a further storey to the tower in 1369 during the civil war which he waged against his step-brother Pedro the Cruel. Nowadays it houses the Museum of the Three Cultures with exhibitions and an audio-visual presentation explaining how daily life might have been in Córdoba when it was a multi-religious, cosmopolitan mediaeval city.

Photograph by Lewis, 1891.

The walls of mediaeval Córdoba were built upon the old Roman wall and during the final years of the caliphate were 22 kilometers long, encompassing an area of some 5,000 hectares. There were seven gates; according to Dr. Juan B. Carpio, starting from the south-east and going clockwise, these were: the Roman Bridge Gate (the Triumphal Arch), across which the Via Augustina ran; then came the XIV century Sevilla Gate, the Almodóvar Gate, the Gate of the Gallicians, the Cemetery Gate (Gate of the Jews, of Talavera ...), the Toledo Gate (The Iron Gate, Gate to Rome, St. Salvador ...), and coming round towards the east once more, the Zaragoza Gate (New Gate). The Sevilla and Almodóvar Gates are flanked by statues of Córdoba's most eminent philosophers Averroës (left) and Seneca.

• **AVERRÖES.** *Author of scholarly treatises on medicine, mathematics, astronomy, ethics and above all philosophy, which had a deep influence on Christian Europe of the time.*

THE CITADEL.

In 1328 Alfonso XI ordered the construction of a Christian fortified palace upon the remains of earlier Roman and Arab buildings close to the mosque. It was to be known as the House of the Christian Monarchs in order to distinguish it from a similar citadel in the vicinity which had been the palace of the Muslim caliphs. It is a square fortress with towers at each corner and encircled within by a gallery flanked by numerous valuable archaeological treasures, among

which are a well-preserved, third-century marble Roman sarcophagus with portraits of the dead and their protecting spirits carved upon it (below). In the great hall, decorated throughout

•THE ALCÁZAR MUSEUM.
This living museum contains various artefacts from Roman times and some tessellated floors found beneath that of the present-day Plaza de la Corredera. Also to be seen here are the well-preserved Islamic steam baths and a Mudéjar courtyard. Surrounding the museum are traditional Moorish-Andalucían gardens with many examples of local flora.

with mosaics, there are likenesses of Polyphemus and Galatea, justly famous for their beautiful colouring, and some excellent, minutely carved bas reliefs (above right: Pegasus).

THE CASTLE (ALCAZAR) OF TH CHRISTIAN MONARCHS, was buil at the beginning of the XIV centur upon the site of previous royal resi dences, overlooking the rive Guadalquivir. Julius Caesar himsel had lived in a Roman residence there for a short while in 65 B.C. after hi defeat of Pompey, and later the Córdoban rulers had built their pala ce on the same site, just beside thei Great Mosque. It was not traditiona for Castillian kings to own their own palaces or even to have any fixed residence and possibly for this reason the Trastamaras dynasty decided to fortify themselves here, extending and reforming what was already in place. During the war against Granada in the last quarter of the XV century the Catholic Monarchs Ferdinand and Isabel, made furthe changes to the castle in order to use i as their headquarters. (It was at this time that Queen Isabel, irritated b the continuous squealing of the mechanism´ of the Albolafia wate wheel in the river just opposite, orde red it to be dismantled, much to the detriment of the people of Córdoba) Their daughter Princess María, the future queen of Portugal, was born here and it was also here tha Boabdil, the last Muslim king o Granada, was kept prisoner for a while after being captured in a skir mish near Loja. Bullfights were held in the courtyard in honour of the Prince Don Juan when the Catholic Monarch's most famous and able field commander Gonzálo Fernández de Córdoba, el Grán Capitán, wa present at the royal court. In 1486 Christopher Columbus first showed his plans for his adventure to the Americas to the King and Queen in the throne-room of this palace.

The palace became the seat of the Holy Inquisition in 1482 and remai ned so until it was abolished as recently ago as 1821. Thenceforth i was used as a prison until 1951 when it was restored to life as a museum and centre for public occasions. The Mudéjar courtyard was restored and above all the gardens were returned to their original splendour and are now a marvel of peace and beauty a

• THE TRIUMPH OF ST. RAPHAEL (RIGHT).
• *Below:* THE TOWER OF ST. NICHOLAS DE LA VILLA, *one of Córdoba's most famous towers. Dating from 1496, it was used as the symbol of Córdoba in the World Exhibition in Sevilla in 1992.*

• BELOW: THE TEMPLE OF CLAUDIUS MARCELLUS. *The abundance of Roman relics constantly coming to light gives us some idea of the importance of this capital city of Baetica. Right: the Bridge Gate.*

WALKING AROUND

THE BRIDGE GATE *(Triumphal Arch).* The present-day gate replaced the older one which formed part of the city wall. It was built by Hernán Ruiz at the behest of King Phillip II and is the epitome of Renaissance style. For centuries the TRIUMPH OF ST. RAPHAEL, guardian angel of Córdoba, has presided over the most important public and private squares in the city, witness to the devotion the townspeople feel for their archangel.

In 1651 he is credited with having rid the city of the black death. The most impressive of these statues to St. Raphael is that sculpted by Verdiguier at the end of the XVII century (above), which stands between the Great Mosque and the Roman bridge. The archangel presides majestically over a slim column rising from a figurative, ornate pedestal, typical of the high Baroque period.

THE TEMPLE OF CLAUDIUS MARCELLUS. At the very heart of the city stand the bare pillars (left) reconstituted from what was once a Roman temple bearing the name of

•**BELOW: DIFFERENT COURTYARDS WITHIN THE GARDENS OF THE PALACE OF VIANA.**
Left: main façade.

the founder of the original colony here, later dedicated during the first century B.C. to the newly deified emperor Augustus.

THE CHURCH OF ST. LAWRENCE. After the Christian reconquest in 1236 King Ferdinand III organised the new Christian city into fourteen parishes, which were popularly known as *parroquias fernandinas* in recognition of this fact. Each had its own church, built in the architectural style of the transition towards the Spanish Gothic, although they all retain certain fortress-like features typical of the Roman period. The most outstanding of these *fernandina* churches is that of St. Lawrence (below).

THE PALACE OF VIANA. This palace, built during the XVI century, is an outstanding example of a noble Córdoban mansion. All visitors to Córdoba admire the courtyards tucked into the narrow streets in front of simple town houses, but this mansion can boast of twelve

• A LA IZQUIERDA IGLESIA DE SAN LORENZO

●COURTYARD OF THE OLD CONVENT OF LA MERCED *(Mercy), beside the Square of Christ of the Lanterns).*

●LA TORRE DE LA MAL MUERTA.
This is a flanking tower built onto the main wall of the city in the XV century. Legend has it that It was constructed by a forlorn husband who had killed his wife, suspecting her of adultery, only to find later that she was completely virtuous.

such courtyards and also one of the oldest designed gardens in the city. On show inside is a collection of splendid ceramics and examples of the important Córdoban craft of intricate silver fili-gree (It isn't open during the week-ends).

THE CONVENT OF MERCY (LA MERCED). This convent was also founded by King Ferdinand in the XIII century but was completely reconstructed in 1757 at the height of the Baroque period, to which so many buildings in the city belong, although none of them can rival this one. The façade was painted only 30 years ago, but what is of real interest to the visitor is its beautiful courtyard (above), its grand stairway and above all the church, which contains the finest example of a Baroque altar piece in the whole of Córdoba. The palace is now home to the offices

• **THE COURTYARD OF THE ZOCO** (*Patio del Zoco*), below: (marketplace), is one of the remaining corners of the town to retain the traditional style of Spanish-Moorish building.

• **ABOVE: THE LA PLAZA DE LA CORREDERA,** *originally designed at the end of the XVIII century as a place for public functions, is a closed square in the Castillian style. It has in its time been used for bullfights, theatre, and the burning of "heretics". Nowadays it has been brightened up as a busy urban centre and is often used for street markets and the such.*

• **BELOW** *the Jewish quarter near the Taurine Museum*
•**FACING PAGE,** *The Hospital of St. Hyacinth (XVI century), originally known as the Hospital of St. Sebastian (bellow).*

of the provincial council.

THE CONGRESS PALACE. This conference centre is housed in the old Hospital of St. Sebastian, situated opposite the Great Mosque. Its building, in late flamboyant Gothic style (sometimes also known as Isabeline), was overseen by Hernán Ruiz the elder. Of greatest interest are the cloister and surrounding buildings.

This artist is considered by many to be the painter who captured the soul of Andalucían women, but he has also been criticised by others who consider that he used his talent only to reflect the worst clichés of a tragic Spain wrapped in its own secret self. His daring subjects, above all the frank realism of his nude figures, provoked a considerable degree of scandal in his day and resulted in the rejection of his portrait Vividores del Amor from the Spanish National Exhibition of Fine Arts in 1906.

MUSEUMS OF CÓRDOBA

The most interesting museums in the city are to be found near to the mosque, in the famous Plaza del Potro. The most visited is in fact that devoted to Julio Romero de Torres. The museum is the studio of the artist and shares its entrance through a garden courtyard with the Provincial Museum of Fine Arts alongside it. Both museums occupy the old Charity Hospital, with its fine Renaissance portico. The Romero de Torres Museum itself is both house and museum in which the furniture and ornaments give an authentic feeling of bour-

geois life between the end of the XIX and beginning of the XX centuries in Andalucía. It has on show some of the artist's most famous portraits, including "La Nieta de Trini", "Naranjas y Limones", Cante Jondo", "La Chiquita Piconera" and "El Pecado", among others. In the downstairs rooms

there are photographs of other paintings of his which are in collections elsewhere. The Museum of Fine Arts contains works ranging

statue of a young horse, from which it derives its name. Apart from the museums, amongst the buildings that surround it is the el

• *Above: paintings by* JULIO ROMERO DE TORRES.

• *Paintings from the* MUSEUM OF FINE ARTS.

from the late Gothic to the XX century, including Antonio del Castillo, Valdés Leal, Zurburán, Rusiñol and Zuloaga, amonst many others. La Plaza del Potro (The Square of the Colt) is a long square of great character and nobility with a fountain crowned by el Potro, the

Potro Inn (see the double page overleaf), records of which go back until at least 1435. Cervantes immortalised it in Don Quixote de la Mancha, referring to it as a den of thieves.

The Diocesan Museum of Fine Arts, in what used to be the bishop's palace, contains an outstanding collection of sculptures and paintings from the XIII to the XV centuries and rooms exhibiting more recent Córdoban painters.

• *Courtyard of the*
BISHOP'S PALACE.
Right: the ceiling
of the palace.

• *Courtyard of the*
TAURINE MUSEUM.

●**BRONZE DEER
FROM A FOUN
TAIN AT MADINAT
AZ-ZAHRA.**

THE TAURINE AND POPULAR CRAFTS MUSEUM. This museum is situated in a beautiful XVI century house in the Plaza de Maimonides. The house itself has many enchanting courtyards such as that at the entrance (left). Its exhibitions include numerous memorabilia of famous Córdoban bullfighters and an interesting collection of crafts connected with the bullring.

THE PROVINCIAL ARCHAEOLOGICAL MUSEUM is second only in importance to the National Archaeological Museum in Madrid. It is housed in a Renaissance palace with a splendid façade, which provides a magnificent setting for the artefacts on show: on the ground floor, apart from the gardens and courtyards, are collections of prehistoric,

Roman and Visigothic finds, including interesting pottery and Iberian sculptures, Roman mosaics, high reliefs and sarcophagi and the famous sculpture of the head of Drusus. On the first floor, above an impressive stairway with a Mudéjar coffered ceiling, are a collection of remains from the Muslim and Mudéjar periods, including woodwork from the mosque, a great collection of the surrounds of mediaeval wells, small stone braseros (charcoal-burning household heaters) and a series of ataurique motifs, together with the famous X century bronze deer from a fountain in the royal city of Madinat az-Zahra and a whole range of artefacts from the caliphal period with decorative and architectural objects such as tiles, column bases, imposts and capitals.

CORDOBA

IN FOCUS

THE PROVINCE OF CORDOBA
MEDINAT AZ-ZAHRA

• SIERRA DE LA HOR-
CONERA. *Whitewashed farmhouses peep out through the olive groves lining the roads between Priego, Rute and Iznajar.*

• STREETS AND
COURTYARDS OF
PRIEGO DE CÓRDOBA
The La Villa quarter forms a small labyrinth of narrow streets, its windows closed with elegant wrought-iron grilles overhung with a profusion of flowers.

• MAIN FAÇADE OF
THE ASUNCION
CHURCH AND THE
AURORA IN PRIEGO.

The Province of Córdoba

The north of the Province of Córdoba lies in the heart of the Sierra Morena, deep mountain-lands, home of the native Iberian holm and cork oaks, where sheep and Iberian, black-hoofed pigs forage at their will. This is part of the "acorn area" of western Spain, stretching down to Huelva in the south and running west and northwards through the hillsides of Extremadura to Sala-manca in the north. Its pork products are famous throug-hout Spain, particularly the hams cured in Jabugo and Guijuelo. The most important towns in this part of the province are Pueblo Nuevo-Peñarroya and Fuente Obe-juna (of lit-

erary fame) on the meseta, and Pozo-blanco and Hino-josa in the district of Pedro-ches. The centre of the province is a great cultivated plain contained within the basin of the river Guadalquivir with its riverside towns of Montoro and Palma del Río; green and sparkling in

• **DURING THE FESTIVALS OF THE 3 MAY** *(the Day of the Cross) and Corpus Christi (see above) the old quarter of la Villa in the town of Priego de Córdoba decks itself out with flowers. The parish church of Our Lady of the Assumption was declared a national monument in 1932, particularly because of its Chapel of the Holy Shrine with an XVIII century dome (to the left and on the following page).*

spring, in summer russet with the iridescent yellow glow of sunflowers and the scarlet flash of poppies in the wheat fields. To the south-west the area of fertile plains, sheltered by the foothills of the Horconera, Alcaide, Gaena and Rute mountain ranges with villages such as Luque, Baena,

Doña Mencía, Cabbra, Rute, Iznájar and Priego de Córdoba nestling in their folds, is now a national park. This district forms the western end of the Jaén and Granada mountain chains and is one of the wildest and most beautiful areas in the whole of Andalucía. It is also the place where Spain's finest olive oil is produced. In the far west of the province, between the towns of Lucena and Puente Genil and the wheat fields and the olive groves, lies the district of Montilla, an undulating stretch of greyish marls densely covered in vineyards that produce full-bodied, sweet and dry

• **CASTLE OF ZUHEROS** *founded in the IX century (above).*
• **CASTLE OF LUQUE** *(below).*

white wines, which are justly famous throughout Spain. Although the name of origin of these wines is strictly Montilla-Moriles, the vineyards extend through areas such as Montemayor and climb up the hillsides of Monturque and Espejo, fortified villages that still betray their ancient

• THE IZNAJAR reservoir is fed by the river Genil.

role of strategic military posts during the border wars between Muslims and Christians 800 years ago. Apart from Priego, with its interesting XVIII and XIX artistic heritage, there are other villages in this area, such as Lucena (St. Mathew's Church, above) and Iznájar (above left) and Baena

(below), which have always maintained a strong tradition of local handicrafts, particularly silk weaving, villages which have maintained a quiet prosperity amidst the considerable hardship of rural life in Spain, and nowadays, following their tradition of self sufficiency and local

•HAND-MADE LEATHERWARE. From the time of the caliphs there has been a great tradition of leather-working in Córdoba, and in fact the famous illustrated ceilings in the Alhambra in Granada are painted on Córdoban leather. The craft thrives to this day thanks to Córdoba's saddlers and harness makers.

• La Campiña

To the south of the city extends the campiña, endless gently undulating plains, a sensual land coloured by a thousand hues of green in winter and spring, highlighted by the chasing shadows of clouds flowing northwards from the Atlantic. In May the wheat ripens and the plains are set on fire by scarlet poppies and glowing yellow sunflowers.

To the south the soil becomes light grey and is planted with the vines that climb up the flanks of the mountains to the south-east, where they eventually give way once more to the majestic olive trees of which the Andalucían poet Antonio Machado wrote:

"Campo, campo, campo,
 y entre los olivos
 los cortijos blancos."

•HE CASTLE OF
BELALCAZAR.

• ANDALUCÍA AND
OLIVES. *The olive
tree has flourished
for more than
2,500 years in
these parts.
Nowadays the
regions of Baena,
with 32,000
hectares, and
Priego have had
their official name
of origin
recognised and
lead the world
rankings in terms
of quality.*

agricultural commerce, have managed to produce and sell an olive oil second to none in the world, together with highly palatable wines.

The olives, grapes and cereals, the three basic crops of the Mediterranean basin from time immemorial, are of such quality in this region as to be renowned throughout the oil- and wine-producing lands from here to the Near East.

The town of Baena, apart from being known as "the olive-oil town" is also called "the town of drums": more than 2,000 religious brothers in fierce competition turn Easter week into a thunder of drums and "cry sleep to death" as they enact the scenes of the Passion

of Christ throughout the streets.

From on high the village of Luque is just discernible in the distance, guarded within its cleft in the rock which has protected it for centuries and the sight of which inspired the romantic XIX century traveller and artist David Roberts to make beautifully dramatic engravings of it. Also nearby is the village of Zuheros, which has hung suspended from

these rocky hillsides since the IX century. And in the vicinity of Zuheros is the entrance to the Cueva de los Murciélagos" (the Cave of Bats), which was inhabited continuously from the palaeolithic to the bronze age. Finds from the cave are exhibited in a small but important archaeological museum nearby.

Signs of the importance of Córdoba's role in the history of Spain are to be found in its remotest corners: the village of Almodóvar del Río, for example, with its imposing castle (above) and the Renaissance church of the mountainous cornice of Hinojosa del Duque (below).

•VILLAGES SUCH AS HINOJOSA DEL DUQUE *(below), Pozoblanco and La Rambla have always been famous in the region for their earthenware and even today have around a hundred potteries between them.*

MADINAT AZ-ZAHRA

Abd ar-Rahman III imitated the Abbasid caliphs in Baghdad in building a royal city just outside the city of Córdoba itself. He chose the hill of al-Arus, where he erected a whole palatial town, which took forty years in the building only to survive thirty-four years thereafter. Extant chronicles of the day speak of 10,000 labourers, 6,000 blocks of stone hewn every day, and more than 4,000 columns brought from the four corners of Muslim Spain. These figures, although often taken to be exaggerated, do in fact seem to be confirmed by scholarly and archaeological research. It would appear that al-Hakan himself oversaw the work, both as prince and later as caliph, and that he managed to assimilate and synthesise eastern motifs and

techniques from Syria with Byzantine influences to create a new and exquisite original style peculiar to the height and maturity of Spanish caliphal architecture.

The walls of Madinat az-Zahra measured 1,518 metres from east to west and 745 metres from north to south and the town was situated on three different levels, or terraces, to allow for the steep slope of the land (some 70 metres from top to bottom). The upper terrace was the site of the caliph's palace, from whence he could survey the whole of the town and his court. The middle terrace was given over to houses for important administrators, offices and court buildings and gardens. The lower terrace was where the lesser functionaries, artisans and soldiers lived; it was also the site of markets, public baths and the mosque. In the very centre of the highest terrace was the main hall, surrounded to the east by three chambers designed for official receptions and beyond these an octagonal throne room with eight doors. According to a chronicler of the day, at

•THE GARDEN PAVILION.
Extending before the Royal Reception Hall was a long pool, the remains of which can still be seen (left). The water would have reflected the pavilion and the other buildings surrounding the gardens, just as can be seen in other Muslim palaces.

the centre of the city is the great square of the central terrace with walls 100 metres long. To its north is the pool before the great hall (Salón Rico), also known as the Hall of Abd ar-Rahman III, which is rectangular and comprises five aisles, the three central ones lined by arcades (left) and the other two in naves behind the rear wall of the building. This hall contains the most refined of caliphal decoration, from the adornments of the bases of the columns and the alternating reds and greens of the columns themselves to the very sophisticated honeycombing of the capitals.

• **THE ROYAL RECEPTION HALL (DAR AL-MULK).**
Legend has it that this hall was so elaborately decorated with gold and silver, diamonds and other precious stones that on entering it all visitors, be they royalty, statesmen, poets, scholars, musicians or dancers, were utterly bedazzled by the sunlight playing a game of enchantment with lights and reflections upon them ... arches of ivory and ebony, walls of multicoloured marbles and translucent jasper, the dome of the roof covered with gold and silver tiles and lined with gilded mosaics.

• **X CENTURY DISH.**
The people of al-Andalus made the same kind of lustre pottery that they had brought with them from Iraq, and in Madinat az-Zahra shards of this type of ceramic ware have been found with the characteristic caliphal design inspired by manganese-green fabrics.

• **JALOUSIES.**
The jalousies were made of wood, except for especially sumptuous examples which were ceramic or carved from marble.

•**MADINAT AZ-ZAHRA.** Abd ar-Rahman III built this royal city some eight kilometres from Córdoba for his favourite, Azahara. She missed the snowy mountains of her home in Syria and so Abd ar-Rahman promised her, "It will snow for you, Azahara my love, I shall make it snow for you", and he covered the surrounding hills with white-blossoming cherry and almond trees.

•**THE MOULDED VEGETAL DESIGN** *in the centre of this panel from the frieze on a door jamb is separated into two rows, each bearing five bunches of leaves surrounded by entwined branches of grape vines, which represent the tree of life.*

CAPITAL AND BASE. *The exquisitely worked ornamentation reached its highest point in the carving of the bases and capitals of the columns. The capital is of the Corinthian order and has two tiers of acanthus leaves. The very freely designed vegetal motifs covering the surfaces are deeply incised. The same is true of this reconstructed column base.*

• **THE HOUSE OF THE VIZIERS** (also known as The House of the Army) stands to the north of the royal residences close to the lower portico and next to the five-metre-thick surrounding wall. All the archaeological excavations at Madinat az-Zahra have been conducted only recently during the twentieth century because its precise location was unknown until then, and so only a tiny part of what might lie hidden beneath the ground has been revealed. From what has been unearthed so far, however, it seems that we may be lucky in that later looters were only interested in building materials and might have left a lot of interesting decorative ornamentation and day-to-day artefacts behind.

• **THE MILITARY BARRACKS (DAR AL-YUND).** *A central axis of three long naves precedes through arcades to a portico, which separates them from the residences of the nobility.*

• **CIVILISATION IN CÓRDOBA DURING THE REIGN OF THE CALIPH ABD AR-RAHMAN III.** *Above: a painting by D. Baxeiras (1862 – 1943) depicting a reception of ambassadors from Byzantium at Madinat az-Zahra.*

• **AL MUGIRA'S FLASK.** This marble flask forms part of a series of jars with domed lids which were found at Madinat az-Zahra.

MEDINA ZAHARA

1. Mosque/Cathedral.
2. Conference and Exhibition
   Center.
3. Palace of the Christian
   Monarchs.
4. Bridge Gate.
5. Triumph of St. Raphael
   (statue)
6. Roman Bridge and
   Calahorra Tower.
7. Arab Water Wheels.

8. Old City Walls.
9. Blossom Lane.
10. Old Sinagogue.
11. Bull-fight Museum
    and Souk.
12. Chapel of St.
    Bartholomew.
13. Almodóvar Gate.
14. House of "las Ceas" or
    "el Indiano".
15. Church of the Holy Trinity.

16. Church of St. Nicholas
    "de la Villa".
17. Church of St. Hypolitus.
18. Conservatory
19. Church of St. Victoria.
20. Archaeological
    Museum.
21. Portillo Arch.
22. House of the
    Marquises of Carpio
23. Compañia Church.

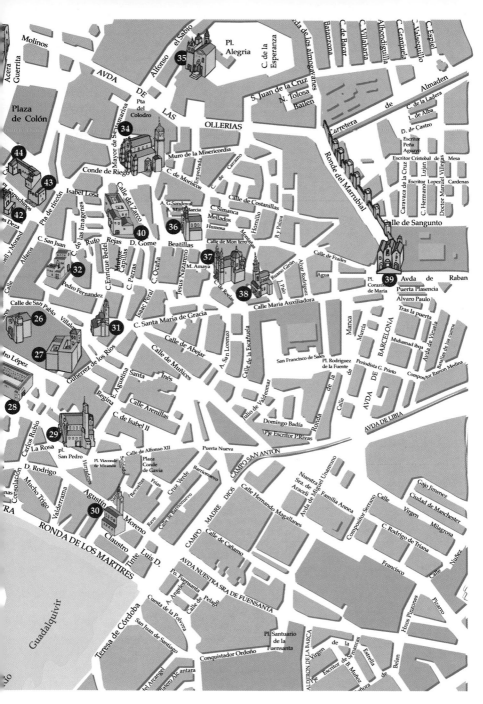

BIBLIOGRAFÍA

AA. VV.: Los andaluces. Istmo, Madrid, 1980.

Acosta Sánchez, José: *Historia y cultura del pueblo andaluz*. Barcelona, 1979.

Cortés Alonso, Vicenta: *Panorama de las fuentes documentales de Andalucía*, en *Actas del Primer Congreso de Historia de Andalucia*, tomo 1.

Cuenca Toribio, José Manuel: Andalucía. *Una introducción histórica*. Córdoba, 1979.

Dominguez Ortiz, Antonio: *Alteraciones andaluzas*. Madrid 1974.

Gomez Moreno, Manuel: *Ars Hispaniae*, (Historia del Arte Medieval) Vol. III. Madrid

Historia del Arte en Andalucia dirigida por Enrique Pareja. Gever. Sevilla 1990

Losada Campos, A.: *Historia de Puente Genil*. Madrid 1971.

Moreno Alonso, Manuel: *Historia General de Andalucia*. Sevilla, 1981.

Nieto Cumplido, Manuel: *La Catedral de Córdoba*. Cajasur, Córdoba. 1998

Ocaña Prados, Juan: *Historia de Villanueva de Córdoba*. Madrid, 1911.

Peláez del Rosal, M., y Rivas Carmona, J.: *Priego de Córdoba*. Salamanca, 1979.

Redondo Guillén, F: *Pozoblanco, capital de Los Pedroches*. Córdoba, 1980.

Valverde Perales, Francisco: *Historia de la villa de Baena*. Toledo, 1903.

Supervisión final: LUIS RECIO MATEO

Published by EDILUX S.L.
Editor: J. Agustín Núñez
Original text: Edilux S.L.
English translation: Jon Trout
Photographs: Miguel Román and J. Agustín Núñez
Photographic composition: EDILUX S.L.
Layout, design and drawings: Estrella Román and Pablo Román
Printing: Copartgraf s.c.a.
Binding: Hermanos Olmedo s.l.
ISBN: 84-87282-41-5
L.D.: GR-736/2001